MONEY SAVVY HAPPY

SYLVIA MILLER-HOWELL
TONY HOWELL

SYLVIA MILLER-HOWELL

Copyright © 2012 SYLVIA MILLER-HOWELL

All rights reserved.

ISBN: 9781090348302

ACKNOWLEDGMENTS

Thank you.

To all of our magnificent clients, past, and present, you have made this book possible by trusting us with the most intimate details of your lives. We are grateful for the opportunity to serve you and help you meet your personal and financial goals.

INTRODUCTION

You have this book; therefore you are serious about making a positive change in your life. This book gives you step by step instructions on how to manage your finances and avoid stress. If our funds are not in order, our entire lives are disrupted.

Money touches every area of our lives, a lack of, or not knowing how to manage your money can cause you to have an unhealthy relationship with your finances.

Our mission is to empower you with education and knowledge to help you get your FIO (Finances In Order).

Welcome!

My people are destroyed for lack of knowledge: because thou hast rejected knowledge, I will also reject thee.

Hosea 4:6 King James Version (KJV)

MONEY SAVVY HAPPY

SYLVIA MILLER-HOWELL

CONTENTS

Acknowledgments

Introduction

Questions	8
What is credit?	12
What is a FICO score?	13
Credit Bureaus	14
How your behavior determines your credit score	15
How the credit bureaus determines your credit score	16
Credit Score Ranges	20
What a low credit score will cost you	22
Building a healthy credit profile	25

CONTENTS

Three steps to increase your credit score	26
Is Credit Repair legal?	27
What to dispute?	29
Letter #1	31
Letter #2	34
Letter #3	36
More Questions	38
How your behavior is evaluated in your credit report?	39
Getting you FIO	40
Budgeting	43
Glossary	47

Introduction Questions

To set the course for the rest of your life and generations to come you must answer the following questions truthfully. This is your personal book, and we encourage you to write in this book. Keep a personal inventory of how you view money, the way you look at money and how you deal with money. Once you have a proper assessment of your outlook on money, our goal is to make sure you are never without it.

Money! Money! Money!

Banks, insurance companies, landlords and employers all look at the way you handle money by reviewing your credit report. This is your report card for the financial world. Usually, people with excellent credit are great money managers.

If you had a Million Dollars what would you do with it?

Do you think having more money will change your circumstances? If so, Why?

_____
_____
_____
_____
_____
_____
_____
_____

Do you have a budget? (Circle one)   yes or no

_____
_____
_____
_____

Are you a shopaholic? (Circle one)   yes or no

_____
_____
_____
_____

Do you buy things to impress others? (Circle one) yes or no

_____
_____
_____
_____

When you go out to lunch/dinner with friends do you always pay everyones bill? (Circle one)   yes or no

_____
_____
_____
_____

When your friends need finances do they come to you or do you volunteer to help? Why?

_____
_____
_____
_____

Can you afford to help your friends financially? (Circle one) yes or no

_____
_____
_____
_____
_____
_____
_____
_____

What is Credit?

Credit is the ability for a person to obtain goods or services before payment. Promising to repay the money for the item received at a later date. If you pay back the money on time your credit score or FICO score will increase.

How much credit do you have?
_____
_____
_____

How much debt do you owe?
_____
_____
_____

Do you use credit cards to buy groceries?
_____
_____
_____

How often do you grocery shop?
_____
_____
_____

Do you make a grocery list?
_____
_____
_____

What is a FICO SCORE?

Do you have a grocery budget? if so, how much?
_____
_____
_____

FICO is a company that mathematically calculates a number to assign to you to gauge your credit worthiness. The name FICO comes from Bill Fair and Earl Issac. They founded The Fair Issac Company in 1956. FICO headquarters is located in San Jose California.

FICO is worth more than $900 million today, it is considered the company the lenders most use to retrieve your credit score for a big ticket item like a mortgage loan. A FICO score is a credit score that is generated by what is now called The Fair Issac Corporation. It is a 3 digit number that can range from 300-800. The higher the score the better your chance of receiving the item on credit with a great interest rate. FICO scores above 680 is considered a good score.

Do you know your FICO score? (Circle one)   yes or no
_____
_____

If so, What is your score?
_____
_____

When did you have someone pull your credit score? Why?
_____
_____
_____

CREDIT BUREAUS

There are several different Credit Bureaus. We have Experian, FICO, Equifax, TransUnion, Innovis and PRBC but today we will only speak about "The Big Three" Experian, TransUnion and Equifax.

These companies collects and maintain your credit information. They sell your information to lenders, creditors and consumers in the form of a credit report. It's like having a report card on your payment history. How you pay? When you pay? And how much credit you have been allotted?

We have TransUnion which is the smallest of the three major Credit Bureaus. The company was created in 1968 by the Union Tank Car Company and the headquarters is now located in Chicago Illinois. Their database contains more than 200 million files. By TransUnion being the smallest of the three they may not have all the information on your credit report that the other two companies have. This is one of the reasons why your scores are different at all the credit Bureaus.

Experian is the largest Consumer Credit Reporting Agency of the three Big Credit Bureaus. They were founded in 1996 and the headquarters is located in Dublin, Republic of Ireland. This company manages the data of 890 consumers and 103 million businesses worldwide.

Equifax is the oldest Consumer Credit Reporting Agency, it was founded in 1899. They analyze more than 800 million businesses worldwide. In 2015 made $2.7 billion in revenue.

Are you familiar with the other credit bureaus?   yes
_____

HOW YOUR BEHAVIOR DETERMINES YOUR CREDIT SCORE?

Do you pay your bills on time? yes or no
_____
_____
_____
_____

How many credit cards do you have?
_____
_____
_____
_____

How you paid your credit cards on time for the last 6 months?
_____
_____
_____
_____

Have you paid your rent on time for the last 6 months?
_____
_____
_____
_____

How long have you had your oldest credit card?
_____
_____
_____
_____

Did you recently close any credit cards? yes or no
_____
_____
_____
_____

How the Credit Bureaus determines your credit score?

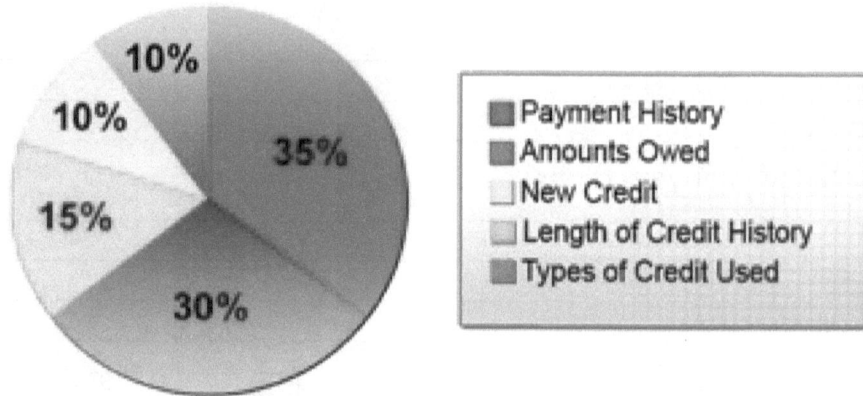

Your payment history accounts for **35%** of your credit score. This is a fairly large amount so if you make your payments late you will lose quite a few points. Anything that is being reported on your credit report must be paid on time. Paying a bill late could cost you anywhere from 40-125 points for one late payment. All bills must be paid on or before the due date. Each individual credit bureau decides how much they will drop your score. There is no set rate for a late car payment or a late house payment, etc.

In determining your overall score, how much money you owe on your bills, accounts for **30%** of your credit score. You should owe less than _____%.

Do you have student loans? If yes, what is the student loan balance?
_____
_____
_____
_____

How many times have you applied for credit in the last 12 months?
_____
_____
_____
_____

The length of time you have been in the credit bureau accounts for **15%** of your credit score. When we say the length of time you have been in the credit bureau we are taking about when you open your first credit card and hopefully you still have it open. If it has not been used in 8 years it may not be on our credit report. You must use your credit cards at least once every 3 months to keep them activated. If you have had your account for 6 years and it was charged off or just left in bad standings we would not take this off of your credit report because it shows the lender that you have had credit in the past even though its bad credit. Bad credit is better than no credit at all.

Next we have new accounts and inquiries. They account for **10%** of your credit score but this can have a major impact on your credit score if you constantly apply for credit. Do not apply for credit within the next 6 to 9 months while you are restoring your credit. When you constantly apply for credit the credit bureaus see you as being desperate and they will continue to lower your score. You should only apply for credit twice in a 12 month period. Every time someone pulls your credit you lose anywhere between three and ten points.

When you go to a car dealership with a not so perfect credit score and apply for a car loan the car salesman will assured you that he will get you into a car. (It only takes 5 mins to pull your credit) but it will take them a while to pull your credit because they not only pulled your credit but they sent the application to 10 other lenders. Well, the payment and the interest rate will be extremely high. If you decide not to get the car and try again in about 2 months your credit score will be worst because that one car dealership has sent your loan application to several other finance companies. Therefore your score may decreased by more than 70 points and you will be in worst shape than you were a couple of months ago.

The last thing you need is a good credit mix, which will account for **10%** of your credit score. Having a good credit mix shows that you are responsible for different types of credit. Lenders favor consumers with a good mix of credit.

You need an **installment loan**, this is a loan with a set payment amount. We suggest you have at least one of the following; Auto loan, mortgage loan, student loan, signature loan or credit builder loan. We highly recommend a credit builder loan from SelfLender. This is the safest way to build your credit score. You would give this company a certain amount every month (as little as $25 a month), in 12 months they will give it back to you with interest. Your score will increase in 3 months if you pay the set payments on time.

Use this referral to open your SelfLender account **https:// selflender.com/refer/19042533**

You will also need a **revolving account**, examples of this type of accounts are: Credit cards issued by a Bank or Credit Union, Credit cards issued by a retail store like Macy's, Walmart, Dillard's etc. Gas credit cards A Home Equity Lines of Credit is also considered a revolving account.

You will also need **open end credit**, this is an account where the entire amount must be paid off in full. An example is your utility bill, your cellular phone bill and some gas cards are paid off in its entirety every 30 days.

It is important to also open a checking account and a savings account at your local bank or credit union.
Do you have a checking account? yes or no
_____
_____
_____
_____

Do you have your paycheck direct deposited into your checking account?
_____
_____
_____
_____

How often do you put money in your savings account?
_____
_____
_____
_____

Do you have a portion of your paycheck direct deposited into your savings account?
_____
_____
_____

CREDIT SCORES RANGES

A less than perfect credit score transcends race, age, location, occupation and gender. This can affect anyone whether the problem is self-inflicted or life experiences has brought you down this path without your control.

- 800 or higher -this score is considered an excellent score. If you walk into a car dealership they will treat you like royalty and you will be given the best interest rate.

- 700-799 - this score is considered very good credit score and you will enjoy great rates, and approved for any type of loan. Your outcome will always be favorable.

- 680-699 - this is consider a good average credit score, you will get approved with a slightly higher interest rate. Try to increase your score to 720 if you are applying for a long term loan because you want the best interest rate possible.

- 620-679 - this is a fair credit rating and your approval depends on your credit history. You may or may not be approved if so you will have high interest rates.

- 580-619 - this is considered poor credit but you can still get an unsecured personal loan and a mortgage. Interest rates will be very high and you can expect to pay more over a long period of time.

- 500-579 - (needs work before applying for anything) you may get this loan but you will have the highest interest rate possible. Proceed with caution, if you decide to get this loan and default you will be in a worst situation.

- 499 or lower - (Don't apply for anything) Take to time to get your finances in order and restore your credit.

Do you know your credit score? If so, what is it?
_____
_____
_____
_____

What a Low Credit Score Will Cost You?

What is your dream car?
_____
_____
_____

How much interest are you willing to pay to get your dream car?
_____
_____
_____

Brand New
2018 Dodge Charger
Cost: $29,090
Term: 60 months

SARAH A. – has a very good credit score therefore, she has an excellent interest rate. She will only pay $1,046.99 in interest during the entire 5 years of her car loan.

- Credit Score: 730
- Interest Rate: 1.4%
- Payment: $502.00
- Total Interest Paid: $1,046.99
- Total Payments: $30,376.79

SARAH B. -- has a low credit score therefore she will pay more than $12,000 in interest by the end of loan.

- Credit Score: 599
- Interest Rate: 14.99%
- Payment: $691.90
- Total Interest Paid: $12,423.78
- Total Payments: $41,513.78

Sarah B. pays $11,376.79 MORE than SARAH A. for the same exact car.

This happens with your credit cards, mortgage, loans etc. Anything you purchase with a low credit score will cost you hundreds of thousands of dollars more than a person with a great credit score.

Your Car insurance will cost more because of your low credit score.

What will you do with $12,000 extra dollars?

~Building a healthy credit profile~

Here are a few things you can do while your credit is being restored

- Open a checking and savings account at a local bank or credit union
- Open a secured loan building account with SelfLender **https://www.selflender.com/refer/19042533** With this account you are lending yourself money and you will received the funds back in 12 months with interest.
- If you are renting you can self-report to TransUnion, Equifax, and Experian.
- Need an installment loan –furniture loan (purchase a small item and pay off in 90 days) would be your best choice. Other installment loans are student loans and auto loans.
- Apply for a secured credit card from your local bank.

3 Steps to increase your credit score immediately

Step 1—Pay all current credit cards down and any revolving credit down to 7%
Step 2—do not close any credit cards,
Step 3—avoid applying for new credit.

Make sure your banking accounts are in good standing. (No overdrafts)

Who do you bank with? Why?
_____
_____
_____

What perks are you getting with your current bank?
_____
_____
_____

Is credit repair legal?

Credit repair is 100% legal and it works *because* of the law. The Fair Credit Reporting Act gives you the right to dispute any item on your credit reports. If an item cannot be verified it must be removed. This will immediately boost your credit score. Even accurate negative items can often be removed or negotiated away.

How does credit repair work?

80% of all credit reports contain errors. This means that most credit reports can be improved instantly. The next step is to work with creditors to negotiate removal of accurate negative items.

Consumer Credit Rights Under State and Federal Law

- You have a right to dispute inaccurate information in your credit report by contacting the credit bureau directly. However, neither you nor a credit repair company or credit repair organization has the right to have accurate, current and verifiable information removed from your credit report. The credit bureau must remove accurate, negative information from your report only if it is over 7 years old. Bankruptcy information can be reported up to 10 years.
- You have a right to obtain a copy of your credit report from a credit bureau. You may be charged a reasonable fee. There is no fee, however, if you have been turned down for credit, employment, insurance, or a rental dwelling because of information in your credit report within the preceding 60 days. The credit bureau must provide someone to help you interpret the information in your credit file. You are entitled to receive a free copy of your credit report if you are unemployed and intend to apply for employment in

the next 60 days, if you are a recipient of public welfare assistance, or if you have reason to believe that there is inaccurate information in your credit report due to fraud.
- You have a right to sue a credit repair organization that violated the Credit Repair Organization Act. This law prohibits deceptive practices by credit repair organizations.
- You have the right to cancel your contract with any credit repair organization for any reason within 3 business days from the date you signed it.
- Credit bureaus are required to follow reasonable procedures to ensure that the information they report is accurate. However, mistakes may occur.
- You may, on your own, notify a credit bureau in writing that you dispute that accuracy of information in your credit file. The credit bureau must then reinvestigate and modify or remove inaccurate or incomplete information. The credit bureau may not charge any fee for this service. Any pertinent information and copies of all documents you have concerning an error should be given to the credit bureau.
- If the credit bureau's reinvestigation does not resolve the dispute to your satisfaction, you may send a brief statement to the credit bureau to be kept in your file, explaining why you think the record is inaccurate. The credit bureau must include a summary of your statement about disputed information with any report it issues about you.
- The Federal Trade Commission regulates credit bureaus and credit repair organizations. For more information contact: The Public Reference Branch Federal Trade Commission Washington, D.C. 20580.

What do I dispute?

Dispute Anything!
- You are legally allowed to dispute anything. If they don't prove it, they must remove it.
- Send a letter to change the address. Get this letter notarize and the address will disappear.
- Send letter to remove inquiries. Letters must be sent to all 3 Credit Bureaus.
- If the items are not removed send another letter.
- If you do not receive a response from the credit bureaus within 45 days by law they must remove the item from your credit report.

The Process
- Send a letter to all 3 credit bureaus requesting your credit reports. (you are entitle to 1 free credit report every 12 months from each credit bureau)
- It could take up to 45 days before the Credit Bureaus respond.
- Be patience…
- This process takes time
- While you are waiting do not apply for credit with anyone
- Do not give anyone your social security number

If you pull your own credit report it will not cost you any points but if someone else pull your credit report you will lose points.

Rebuilding your credit to purchase a home

- The best credit is old credit good or bad.
- How long have you had your credit? Accounts for 15% of your credit score.
- A person with a 2 year credit history will not have the score of a person with a 30 year credit history. Longevity is best when purchasing a big ticket item.
- If you would like to purchase a home do not purchase a car unless you pay cash for the car or have made plans to make the car your home.

LETTER #1   "NOTARIZE"

* You are allowed one free credit report a year
* First letter to send to the credit bureaus

Date: January 23, 2015

From: Sarah B. Good
           800 Credit Score Way
           Anywhere, USA 12345

To: Equifax

Attn:Customer Relations Department

To Whom It May Concern:
My name is _____ my social security number is _____.

Please send a free copy of any credit reports in my name to the following address:

Thank you,

_____
Enc. Driver License, SSN Card, and Proof of Residence

* *Do not put this information on the letter you send to the credit bureaus.*

You've received your credit reports

NOW WHAT!

- Check addresses to make sure the correct address on the reports
- Carefully look at all the information to make sure your creditors are accurate.
- Make sure the amount you owe is correct.
- Check to make sure everything on your credit report belongs to you.

Letter #2

*Send this letter immediately after you receive your credit reports in the mail.

Date: January 23, 2015 (Today's date)

From: Sarah B. Good
        740 Credit Score
        Anywhere, USA 12345

To: Equifax

Attn: Customer Relations Department

Report # _____

To Whom It May Concern:

I am writing to correct my personal information.

Please update my address to:
_____.
Please update my name:
_____.
My only social security number is:
_____.
My correct birthday is:
_____.
My only employer is
_____.

Please remove my telephone number from the reports in my name.

I do not wish to have any telephone numbers on the reports in my name.

Please remove all the other addresses off of the credit report in my name, as they are not deliverable to me by the United States Post Office, and they are not reportable as per the FCRA, since they are inaccurate.

Sincerely,

_____

Enc. Driver License, SSN Card, and Proof of Residence

*** Do not put this information on the letter you send to the credit bureaus.**

Letter #3

*Send this letter immediately after you receive your credit reports in the mail if you have unauthorized Inquiries

* Inquiries are when someone request a copy of your credit report

* If you give anyone your social security number they will pull your credit report.

Date: January 23, 2015 (Today's Date)

From: Sarah B. Good
        740 Credit Score
        Anywhere, USA 12345

To: Equifax

RE: Request for Investigation of Unauthorized Inquiry
Report #_____

To Whom It May Concern,

I checked my personal credit report, which I acquired from your organization on Date_____ and I noticed that this unauthorized inquiry had been made:

I am requesting your help in resolving this matter.

In accordance with the Fair Credit Reporting Act, I request you immediately initiate an investigation into this inquiry on my credit report to determine who authorized the inquiry. If, once your investigation is complete, you find my allegation to be true, please remove the unauthorized inquiry from my credit report and send me an updated copy of my credit report at my address listed above. If you do find the inquiry referenced above to be valid, I request that you please send me a full description of the procedures used in your investigation within 15 business days of the completion of the investigation.

Thank you for your help and assistance.

Sincerely,

_____

Enc. Driver License, SSN Card, and Proof of Residence

* ***Do not put this information on the letter you send to the credit bureaus.***

Why in the Richest Country in the World Americans are living Paycheck to Paycheck?

Are you one paycheck away from being homeless?

Do you live paycheck to paycheck? Why?

How your behavior is evaluated in your credit report

Honesty is the only way to make changes. You must be honest with yourself. Answer the following questions

- Do you pay your bills on time?
- Are you late on your rent?
- How much will it cost you if you pay your rent late?
- Do you pay your utility bill on time?
- Did the utility company ask for a deposit when you started service with them?
- How much do you pay in late fees per month for paying your bills late?
- What interest rate are you paying on your car?
- How much do you owe on your car?
- Do you think you paid too much for your car?
- How much do you pay for car insurance for one year?
- Are your credit cards maxed out?
- How long have you been renting?
- How much have you paid in rent in the last 12 months?
- How long have you had your accounts?
- Did you recently close any credit card?
- How many times have you applied for credit in 12 months?_____.

After carefully answering the above questions how well are you managing your finances?
_____
_____
_____
_____

Getting Your FIO (Finances In Order)

To get our (FIO) Finances In Order we must have a budget and know what funds we have coming in and what funds are going out.

We must give every dollar a place. We should always know what purpose every dollar will serve before you receive your money.

1. How Often do you receive a paycheck or funds?
A. Daily
B. Weekly
C. Bi-weekly
D. Twice a month
E. Monthly

2. How often do you receive other income?
A. Daily
B. Weekly
C. Bi-weekly
D. Twice a month
E. Monthly

3. How often do you receive funds from child support?
A. Daily
B. Weekly
C. Bi-weekly
D. Twice a month
E. Monthly

4. How often do you receive funds from other sources?
A. Daily
B. Weekly
C. Bi-weekly
D. Twice a month
E. Monthly

WEEKLY

If you receive your paycheck weekly use the formula below to calculate your monthly income. This calculation is for the money that you bring home on your weekly paycheck which is your net income. The gross income is the amount before your taxes, medical etc. is taken from your check.

If your check is $550 a week you would times $550 by 52 weeks (# of weeks in a year).

$550 x 52 = $28,600 (this is your annual income)

Take the annual income of $28,600 divide it by 12 (# of months in a year).

$28,600 ÷ 12 = $2,383

Total monthly income - $2,383 (pay your bills first)

BI-WEEKLY

If you receive your paycheck bi-weekly use the formula below to calculate your monthly income. This calculation is for the money that you bring home on your bi-weekly paycheck which is your net income. The gross income is the amount before your taxes, medical etc. is taken from your check.

If your check is $1191 on the 15th and 30th of every month, you would times $1191 by 24.

$1191 x 52 = $28,584 (this is your annual income)

Take the annual income of $28,584 divide it by 12 (# of months in a year).

$28,584 ÷ 12 = $2,382

Total monthly income - $2,382 (pay your bills first)

MONTHLY

If you receive your paycheck weekly use the formula below to calculate your monthly income. This calculation is for the money that you bring home on your weekly paycheck which is your net income. The gross income is the amount before your taxes, medical etc. is taken from your check.

If your check is $2383 once a month, you would times $2383 by 12 months (# of months in a year).

$2383 x 12 = $28,596 (this is your annual income)

Take the annual income of $28,596 divide it by 12 (# of months in a year).

$28,596 ÷ 12 = $2,383

Total monthly income - $2,383 (pay your bills first)

Budgeting

Make a list of all your bills, amount and due date.
Place the bill on the number of day it is due.

1. _Example:Rent $ 800_
2. _____
3. _____
4. _____
5. _____
6. _____
7. _____
8. _____
9. _____
10. _____
11. _____
12. _____
13. _____
14. _____
15. _____
16. _____
17. _____
18. _____
19. _____
20. _____
21. _____
22. _____
23. _____
24. _____
25. _____
26. _____
27. _____
28. _____
29. _____
30. _____
31. _____

Total of all your bills-_____

Now take a calculator and add.
Place your income on the appropriate date.

1. _____
2. _____
3. _____
4. _____
5. _____
6. _____
7. _____
8. _____
9. _____
10. _____
11. _____
12. _____
13. _____
14. _____
15. _____
16. _____
17. _____
18. _____
19. _____
20. _____
21. _____
22. _____
23. _____
24. _____
25. _____
26. _____
27. _____
28. _____
29. _____
30. _____
31. _____
Total of all income-_____

Combine Income and Bills on the appropriate date.

1. _____
2. _____
3. _____
4. _____
5. _____
6. _____
7. _____
8. _____
9. _____
10. _____
11. _____
12. _____
13. _____
14. _____
15. _____
16. _____
17. _____
18. _____
19. _____
20. _____
21. _____
22. _____
23. _____
24. _____
25. _____
26. _____
27. _____
28. _____
29. _____
30. _____
31. _____

Take Total Monthly Income _____

FROM

Total Monthly Bills_____

Balance_____

Your balance is the amount you have left after you pay all your bills.

Pay your bills first.

GLOSSARY

Bank - A bank is a financial institution licensed to receive deposits and make loans.

Behavior - The way in which a person conducts themselves and their finances.

Beyond your means - Spending more money than what you receive in your income.

Bills - Debt you owe to someone else.

Budget - Allowing a certain amount of money to spend.

Change - Doing something a different way.

Checking account - an account at a bank, in which checks can be drawn on.

Confidence - Feeling certain about something.

Credit - Getting goods and/or services without immediate payment. Pay later on a schedule.

Credit Bureau - A company that collects information to determine your credit worthiness.

Credit Cards - A small plastic card issued by banks or businesses: allowing the cardholder to purchase goods and/or services on credit.

Credit Repair - Is the process of removing negative items from your credit report.

Credit Union - A financial institution created and operated by members and profits shared amongst the owners.

Dispute - a disagreement

Evaluate - To examine someone or something.

Finances In Order (FIO) - A budgeting program Breac Consulting uses to help you get your finances in order.

FICO - Fair Issac Corporation; A company used by most lenders to calculate your credit score when purchasing a home.

Habits - When a person does the same thing repeatedly; over and over again.

Inquiry - When a creditor pulls your credit this is called an inquiry, because they are inquiring about your credit worthiness.

Installment Loan - this is a loan with set payments on a set schedule.

Interest Rate - the amount the lender charges you for borrowing money.

www.ingramcontent.com/pod-product-compliance
Lightning Source LLC
Chambersburg PA
CBHW030736180526
45157CB00008BA/3191